Get Wise

Violence

➡ why does it happen?

Sarah Medina

www.heinemann.co.uk/library

Visit our website to find out more information about **Heinemann Library** books.

To order:
☎ Phone 44 (0) 1865 888066
🗎 Send a fax to 44 (0) 1865 314091
💻 Visit the Heinemann Bookshop at www.heinemann.co.uk/library to browse our catalogue and order online.

First published in Great Britain by Heinemann Library, Halley Court, Jordan Hill, Oxford OX2 8EJ, part of Harcourt Education.

Heinemann is a registered trademark of Harcourt Education Ltd.

Editorial: Lucy Thunder and Harriet Milles
Design: David Poole and Kamae Design
Illustrations: Jeff Anderson
Picture Research: Melissa Allison and Kay Altwegg
Production: Camilla Smith

Originated by Ambassador Litho Ltd
Printed and bound in China, by WKT Company Limited

The paper used to print this book comes from sustainable resources.

ISBN 0 431 21034 9
09 08 07 06 05
10 9 8 7 6 5 4 3 2 1

British Library Cataloguing in Publication Data
Medina, Sarah
(Get Wise). – Violence – why does it happen?
303.6

A full catalogue record for this book is available from the British Library.

Acknowledgements
The Publishers would like to thank the following for permission to reproduce photographs:
p. **4** Bubbles/Ian West; p. **6** Alamy/John Powell; pp. **7, 14** www.JohnBirdsall.co.uk; p. **8** Alamy/Robert Harding; pp. **9, 19, 21, 27** Alamy/Royalty Free; p. **10** Alamy/Shout; p. **12** Bubbles/Peter Sylent; p. **13** Alamy/Janine Wiedel Photolibrary; p. **15** Alamy; p. **16** Alamy/Ian Thraves; p. **17** Bubbles/Hercules Robinson; p. **18** Bubbles/David Robinson; p. **20** Corbis/Benjamin Lowy; p. **22** Action Plus; p. **23** Action Plus/Richard Francis; p. **24** Press Association/Tim Ockenden; p. **25** Bubbles/Angela Hampton; p. **26** Photofusion/Paula Solloway; p. **28** Bubbles/John Powell; p. **29** Getty Images/Photodisc

Talk time images pp. **5, 7, 9, 11, 25, 28** Getty Images/Photodisc

Cover photograph reproduced with permission of Associated Press

The Publishers would like to thank Dr Ute Navidi, former Head of Policy at ChildLine for her assistance in the preparation of this book.

Every effort has been made to contact copyright holders of any material reproduced in this book. Any omissions will be rectified in subsequent printings if notice is given to the Publishers.

Disclaimer
All the Internet addresses (URLs) given in this book were valid at the time of going to press. However, due to the dynamic nature of the Internet, some addresses may have changed, or sites may have changed or ceased to exist since publication. While the author and Publishers regret any inconvenience this may cause readers, no responsibility for any such changes can be accepted by either the author or the Publishers.

Important note: If you are living with violence, and you are very upset or feel that you can't cope, go straight to the Getting help box on page 31. There are phone numbers to call for immediate help and support.

Contents

Words appearing in bold, **like this**, are explained in the Glossary.

A violent world

What do we mean by violence?

What do we see in the world around us? There are many good people, who do good things every single day. But there is also a lot of violence, with some people acting badly towards others. Violence is when somebody uses force or power against somebody else, and hurts them in some way.

Getting physical

Have you ever seen anyone hit, kick or push someone else – at school, perhaps? This is **physical violence**. Some people who use physical violence may even use weapons, such as knives or guns. Physical violence is dangerous and can cause serious injury and even death.

Drivers sometimes react ⬆ violently if they feel that someone else has been driving badly.

Just words?

Sometimes, people use words to hurt someone else's feelings. This is called **emotional violence**. **Bullies** often use emotional violence, for example, by calling their **victims** names or ignoring them on purpose.

Violence all around us?

Violence happens everywhere – in homes and schools, in local communities, and in and between different countries. Perhaps you yourself have felt like shouting at or hitting someone – especially if something does not go your way.

Talk time

Where do we see or hear about violence?

 Scott: Some films at the cinema are violent.

 Lei-Lei: TV programmes sometimes show violence, too.

Rick: Yeah – like the news. And soaps!

 Tanvi: Some computer games are violent; you have to fight and kill each other.

Newsflash

An Action Man advert has been banned from being shown on British TV before 9pm, because it is too violent. The ad shows an Action Man doll slicing off his enemy's arms. Even though the chopped-off arm was obviously not real, the ad was not suitable for young children because there were real people in it, as well as toys.

Staying safe

Violence can be very frightening. Fortunately, many people are working hard to protect you from violence. There is a lot you can do, too, to avoid violence and to stay safe. This book will give you lots of help and ideas.

FRIENDLY GAME:
England
v
France

REF

Where might you come across violence?

It is a sad fact that most people will come across violence at some point in their lives. Perhaps you have been a **victim** of violence yourself, or perhaps you know someone else who has.

Falling out

Some children have to face violent behaviour at home, or at school or in their community. Sometimes friends fall out and say or do hurtful things. Even playing can sometimes turn violent, if teasing or play-fighting gets out of hand. Hitting, kicking or pushing another person – or hurting them in some other way – is never acceptable.

Fact flash

About one in twelve pupils in the UK, and one in six pupils in Australia is bullied every week.

Bullies sometimes ➲ physically attack their victims. This kind of violence – like all violence – is unacceptable.

Big bullies

Bullying is one of the most common forms of violence. Most people know someone who is a bully or who has been bullied. Bullies will often call their **victims** horrible names. Sometimes they use **physical violence**, too – and this can be dangerous. For example, pushing someone over could make them hit their head, and they could get badly hurt.

Talk time

Have you ever come across violent behaviour?

 Rick: On the way to school one day, I saw this older boy pushing someone and pinching their stuff. It was really scary.

Lei-Lei: Yeah, a girl in my class used to really bully this other girl. She made her cry.

 Scott: This older boy kept calling me names – just because I don't look the same as him.

Tanvi: Yes, people can be really cruel sometimes.

Getting angry and shouting always makes things worse. Try talking it over quietly instead.

THINK IT THROUGH

Is fighting back ever a good idea?

Yes. If someone hits you, you have to hit them back to make them stop.

No. Fighting back just makes things worse. It's better to walk away – or ask an adult to help.

What do YOU think?

why are people violent?

What kind of things make people want to use violence?

Have you ever felt really angry about something? When people lose their tempers, they sometimes shout or hit out at the person they are angry with. Perhaps they think that this might sort things out, or maybe they just want to make themselves feel stronger and more powerful. They may feel so angry that they lose control of their own behaviour.

Drinking too much ⊙ alcohol may make people act violently. But being drunk is no excuse for hitting out.

Under pressure

Sometimes, people who act violently are unhappy because they are stressed. They may feel out of control because they have lost their job and have no money, or because they are worried about something. This might make them less able to stay in control of their emotions.

Feel the power

Being in a gang can sometimes lead people to act violently, because of **peer pressure**. It can be hard not to do something when all your friends are doing it! When they are together, gang members sometimes drink **alcohol** and use **drugs**. This may make them more likely to use violence.

Learning it

It is possible to learn to be violent. If children see their parents acting violently, or watch violence on TV, they might use violence themselves when they have a problem. It is far better to learn that violence is not the answer!

No excuse!

People act violently for all sorts of reasons – but there is never any excuse for violence. There are always other ways that people can deal with their problems or angry feelings. Taking them out on another person is not the answer!

Talk time

What should you do if you feel really angry with someone?

Tanvi: You should try to stay cool, even if you feel angry.

Scott: Talking is best. If you can tell the person what you are feeling, without shouting, that will help them to understand.

Lei-Lei: Yeah, if you start calling them names or yelling at them, they'll just get angry, too!

Rick: You should always try to listen to their point of view. You can't always be in the right!

❶ People who hang around in gangs can be more likely to get involved in violent situations.

THINK IT THROUGH

Can there ever be any excuse for violent behaviour?

Yes. Sometimes, it's not your fault – especially if you get so angry that you can't control your temper.

No. Violence hurts other people. No matter how bad you feel, you should never take it out on others.

What do YOU think?

Just a smack?

Is smacking children a form of violence?

Violence hurts people in many different ways – and it is never acceptable. However, sometimes there is a question mark over what is violence and what isn't – especially when it comes to parents and their children.

To smack or not to smack?

In many countries, including the UK and Australia, parents sometimes smack their children if they have done something wrong. Many people believe that smacking teaches children to do what is right. Others say that smacking is violence, just like any other kind of violence. They say that there is no difference between an adult hitting another adult and an adult hitting their child.

Smacking no more?

In some countries, such as Sweden, it is **illegal** to smack children – even if you are the child's parents. In the UK and Australia, teachers and childminders are **banned** from smacking the children they look after. People who are against smacking say that it does not teach children to behave better. In fact, they say that smacking teaches children to use violence as a way to sort out their own problems.

Top thoughts

'A smack is parents trying to hit you but, instead of calling it a hit, they call it a smack.'

Seven-year-old girl

❶ Many people believe that parents should not be allowed to smack their children.

Talk time

Should parents and **carers** be banned from smacking their children?

Rick: Definitely! If your parents really care about you, they won't smack you.

Tanvi: Yeah, but what if you don't listen to them when they just talk to you?

Scott: They could always ground you.

Lei-Lei: Sometimes, my mum stops my spending money for a week if I've done something wrong. I hate that!

Newsflash

Reports show that children can be seriously hurt by parents who smack them. A group of **MPs** and children's **organizations** are trying to get the UK **government** to ban parents from smacking their children. But the government does not want to ban smacking completely. Instead it says that smacking will only be **illegal** if it causes bruises or red marks on the skin.

*'I'll teach **YOU** not to say no to ice-cream for breakfast!'*

THINK IT THROUGH

Is smacking children OK?

Yes. If children are very naughty, it may be the only way to make them behave better.

No. Smacking hurts, and no one should be allowed to use violence against anyone else.

What do **YOU** think?

All in the Family

What is domestic violence?

We have seen that parents sometimes smack their children for doing the wrong thing – and that many people believe that smacking should be **banned**. Smacking may or may not be called 'violence' – but, in some families, other kinds of serious violence can take place. Children or other adults in the family can be the **victims** of this violence.

Over the top

Some parents may be too strict with their children, or they may find it hard to control their temper. They may use **physical violence** that is much worse than a smack. Some parents use **emotional violence** to control their children. Perhaps they call them horrible names or tell them they are stupid. This is wrong, and children who are suffering violence like this need to get help from other adults who care about them.

Children often hear ➲ domestic violence going on, no matter how hard they try to get away from it.

Domestic violence

Domestic violence is normally when one adult in the home is violent towards another adult in the family – usually their wife, husband or partner. It is mainly men who are violent towards women in the home – but it can be the other way round, too. In some families, domestic violence may happen every week – or just sometimes.

Domestic violence is often physical – but it can be emotional, too. Victims of domestic violence may be **threatened** or called horrible names. No matter how hard they try, they cannot do anything 'right'. This can make them feel very frightened and lonely.

Everybody hurts

Many people are too afraid or embarrassed to talk about domestic violence. The whole family is affected by it, and it can be very scary to live with. If you are living with domestic violence, it is important to get help. Remember – domestic violence is never your fault, and you do not have to suffer alone.

Domestic violence is frightening, and the whole family needs help to deal with it.

THINK IT THROUGH

Is it OK for people to lose their tempers with members of their family?

Yes. It is normal to get really angry if someone has done something you don't like.

No. People might feel angry about something – but they should not lose their temper, because this could lead to domestic violence.

What do YOU think?

Any excuse for violence?

Why does domestic violence happen?

Domestic violence is a horrible thing, which hurts everyone in the family. There are many reasons why people are violent to the people they are supposed to love – but no one should ever use these as an excuse.

Power games

Some people use violence to make themselves feel stronger. They do not care about other people's feelings. All they care about is being the boss. Just think about **bullies** at school – they often just want to be seen to be cool or 'big', and they do this by hurting someone else.

The only way...?

Children who were brought up with violence in their family sometimes think that violence is normal. When they become adults, they may use violence too. However, many children decide that they will never use violence when they grow up – because they know just how much it hurts.

Fact Flash

One in four women experience domestic violence at some time in their lives.

☞ Some children who live with domestic violence may believe that violence is 'OK', and so they act violently, too.

Too much stress

Sometimes, stress can be a cause of domestic violence. For example, if someone loses their job, they may feel that they have lost control over their life. Controlling somebody else through domestic violence may make them feel better about themselves.

All drugged up

Some **drugs**, including **alcohol**, can make some people more violent. Domestic violence often happens when someone is drunk. The next day, they may feel terrible that they have hurt someone they love – but when they are drunk, they do not care.

Jake's story

Jake knows that alcohol can lead to domestic violence.

'It used to happen every Friday night. Dad would go out with his mates to the pub, and come home drunk. When he got home, if there was any mess around the house, he would go mad. He'd shout at Mum, and then start throwing things around. Sometimes, he hit her. I saw Mum a few times with a black eye, and he even broke her nose once. I hated him for doing that.'

🎧 Drinking too much alcohol is one of the causes of domestic violence.

THINK IT THROUGH

Does being violent really make you stronger?

Yes. You can make people do what you want if you are violent – so you feel stronger.

No. People who are violent are not strong, because they cannot control themselves.

What do YOU think?

What is it like to live with domestic violence?

Domestic violence does not just affect the person who is being physically hurt. Living with domestic violence is awful for the whole family.

Not in front of the children?

Children who live with **domestic violence** cannot hide from it. They often see the violence happening. Even if they get out of the way – by going to their bedroom, for example – they can usually hear what is going on. Afterwards, they may see any injuries, such as bruising, that have been caused. This can be very frightening.

Stop!

Sometimes, children try to stop one adult from hurting another, by shouting or crying, or even by getting in the middle. By doing this, they may get hurt themselves.

Even if children do not ➔ see violence happening, the signs may be clear enough the next day.

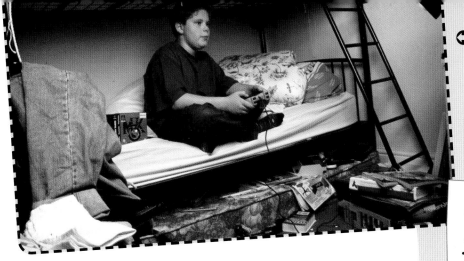

Young people often feel that if they kept their rooms tidier and did everything right, the violence might stop. The truth is: domestic violence is never their fault.

Sssshhhh...

Many people who are **victims** of domestic violence do not want other people to know about it. They may ask their children to keep it a secret. This can make everyone feel even more frightened and ashamed.

All too much

It is horrible when you love both your parents or **carers**, but one of them is hurting the other. It is normal to feel scared, confused and upset. Some children find it hard to sleep or study. Older children may find that their younger brother or sister starts wetting the bed, or has tummy aches. Some children feel that no one loves or cares about them.

Kalifa's story

Kalifa and her brother didn't know how to cope with their mum's violence towards their dad:

'My mum used to hit my dad. It sounds stupid, because Dad just let her. I think he didn't want to hurt her back. My brother and I weren't allowed to talk about it. We didn't even talk to each other. We just tried to pretend it wasn't happening. I used to cry myself to sleep when I heard Mum and Dad arguing. I felt so angry and stupid, because I couldn't stop it.'

THINK IT THROUGH

Is telling ever wrong?

Yes. If someone asks you to keep a secret, you are breaking a promise if you tell.

No. Telling someone about domestic violence is important. It can help to keep you and other people safe.

What do YOU think?

How can you deal with domestic violence?

Living with **domestic violence** can feel very lonely and frightening. It is important to remember that you are not alone. Many people know what you are going through, because they have gone through it themselves.

Talk it over

Talking things over with someone you trust can help you to deal with domestic violence. This could be a family member, such as a grandparent, or a teacher at school. Just sharing your feelings will start to make you feel better.

Staying safe

If you see domestic violence at home, do not try to get in the way – because you may get hurt. If you can, leave the room. If you feel in any kind of danger, you should phone a family friend or neighbour – or the police – for help (see page 31).

Top thoughts

'I'm glad my father left us. He put my mother and me through some real **abuse**.'

Christina Aguilera

Some children's ➲ **organizations** have websites where you can find out how to get help.

Walking away

Sometimes, the only way for domestic violence to stop is for one of the adults to leave the family home. But the **victim** of violence may feel too scared to leave, or they may still love the person who is hurting them. They may also believe that the violence will stop. People who hurt their loved ones often promise that they will never do it again. However, domestic violence usually gets worse, not better.

If your mum is a ➡ victim of domestic violence, perhaps you could show her the phone numbers on page 31 where she can get help.

THINK IT THROUGH

Should you try to step in to stop domestic violence?

Yes. If you don't try to stop the violence, someone could get badly hurt.

No. You should never step in because you could get hurt yourself. It is always better to phone another adult for help.

What do YOU think?

What is the effect of showing violence in the media?

Even if we do not see violence in our day-to-day lives, we can often see it in the **media**. Have you ever watched TV programmes or played computer games where people fight and hurt each other? Perhaps you have seen newspapers or news programmes showing people who have been killed? This can be very upsetting.

Child protection

Most parents and **carers** want to protect children from media violence. In some countries, TV programmes containing violence can only be shown after a certain time at night. Films have certificates, such as PG (Parental Guidance), to try to make sure that children and young people do not watch things that are bad for them.

Every day brings ➲ more stories of violence in our media.

Violence breeds violence?

Many experts think that watching violent programmes or playing violent games makes children more violent. In the UK in 1993, two ten-year-olds killed a little boy called Jamie Bulger after they had watched a very violent film. In the USA, some students have used guns to hurt and kill other students. People believe that this is partly because they have seen too much violence in the media.

Under pressure?

Have you ever watched films or played games that contained violence, just because your friends were doing it? Remember, if you don't like it, you can choose to say 'No'. Violence is not cool – and it is never funny.

Newsflash

A recent study says that young people find news pictures more upsetting than other violent scenes on television. The study showed that children could easily see the difference between made-up violence in TV shows and cartoons, and the real thing. Children were most worried by violence involving other children. Some people now believe that viewers should be told in advance when news reports featuring violent scenes are going to be shown on TV.

◀ Some computer games may make violence out to be exciting and even fun. But, in real life, violence is just the opposite.

THINK IT THROUGH

Should TV programmes have warnings if they are going to show violence?

Yes. That way, you do not have to see the violence, if you don't want to.

No. Violence is all around us, anyway – so what's the point?

What do YOU think?

Is violence a normal part of sport?

Have you ever seen anyone lose their temper in games or sports matches? Sometimes, players push each other – or even hit or kick out at the people they are playing against. This is completely wrong, because sport is meant to be fun!

Purely professional?

Some people think that violence in **professional** sport is becoming part of the game itself. Footballers are often sent off the pitch during matches for using **physical violence** against other players, or the referee. In big tennis events, some tennis players have had to pay **fines** for using violent language against the umpire.

Tennis is not normally ➲ known for violence – but more and more players are having to pay fines because they lose their tempers at matches.

Fun to watch?

Some people believe that sports professionals who use violence during games can encourage their fans to be violent, too. Some football fans like to fight each other before, during or after matches. Perhaps they prefer the violence to the sport itself? But it just spoils the match for everyone, and can be very dangerous.

⟲ Violence between different groups of football fans can be a serious problem at some matches.

THINK IT THROUGH

Do sports people encourage their fans to act violently?

Yes. If sports people are violent with each other, fans will use violence too.

No. Everybody can choose whether to be violent or not. You just have to walk away from violence.

What do YOU think?

Top thoughts

'Booing the national anthem, **racism** and jumping on the pitch has to stop. Just get behind the team and do it in a nice way ...'

David Beckham,
England footballer

Keeping cool

How do you stop yourself from being violent if you get angry?

Everybody gets angry sometimes. Anger is a natural feeling, like love and happiness. If your brother or sister takes something without asking you, you might feel angry. You may feel angry if your mum asks you to clean your room when you want to watch TV. Feeling angry for a while may be OK – but only as long as you do not use **physical violence** or **emotional violence** against other people.

Paying the price

Everything we do has a **consequence**. If you say horrible things to your friend because you are angry, they might not hang out with you any more. If you hit someone at school, you will get into trouble with your teacher. People who are violent can get into serious trouble with the police, too. It is much better to learn how to deal with angry feelings in a way that does not hurt anyone.

◑ Having some 'time out' to work out your thoughts and feelings is the best way to deal with anger.

TOP TIPS

If you get angry with someone, always try to give yourself some time to calm down before you say or do anything:

◎ Try taking a few deep breaths.

◎ Spend some time on your own for a while. Later, you can say what you feel without shouting.

◎ Always try to think about how the other person is feeling – and listen to what they have to say.

◎ If you feel like hitting someone, try hitting a pillow instead – it is much better for everyone!

◎ If you still feel angry, talk to an adult about it. They may be able to help you.

Talk time

What could you do to calm down if you feel angry?

Lei-Lei: You could count to ten slowly!

Rick: Or you could just go and do something else until you feel better.

Scott: Yeah, like listen to some music or read a book – or kick a ball around!

Tanvi: You could write down why you're feeling angry, too.

Rick: And maybe talk to someone about it.

THINK IT THROUGH

Is it always possible to keep cool?

Yes. It's up to you whether you lose your temper or not. No one can make you be violent.

No. Sometimes, you might feel so angry that you can't keep cool. That is not your fault.

What do YOU think?

Newsflash

Girls Aloud singer, Cheryl Tweedy (below), punched a toilet attendant in a nightclub after she lost her temper. The attendant said that Cheryl got violent when she asked Cheryl to pay for some sweets she was selling. The singer had to do 120 hours' unpaid work in the community as a punishment, and she also had to pay a **fine**.

In the eyes of the law

How does the law help to protect people from violence?

Violence is wrong. It is always damaging – and it can be very dangerous. Because of this, most countries have **laws** to protect people against violence.

It's my right!

Everybody has **rights** – including you! Rights are things that you can and should expect. Some of these rights are written down as laws. If you know your rights, it will help you to be sure that nobody has the right to treat you badly. It will also remind you that you can ask for help whenever you need it.

You have the right:

- to be loved
- to be safe
- not to be **abused** in any way
- to ask for – and to receive – help whenever you need it.

Fact Flash

Assault is when someone punches, kicks or pushes another person, without causing serious injury. Assault is against the law.

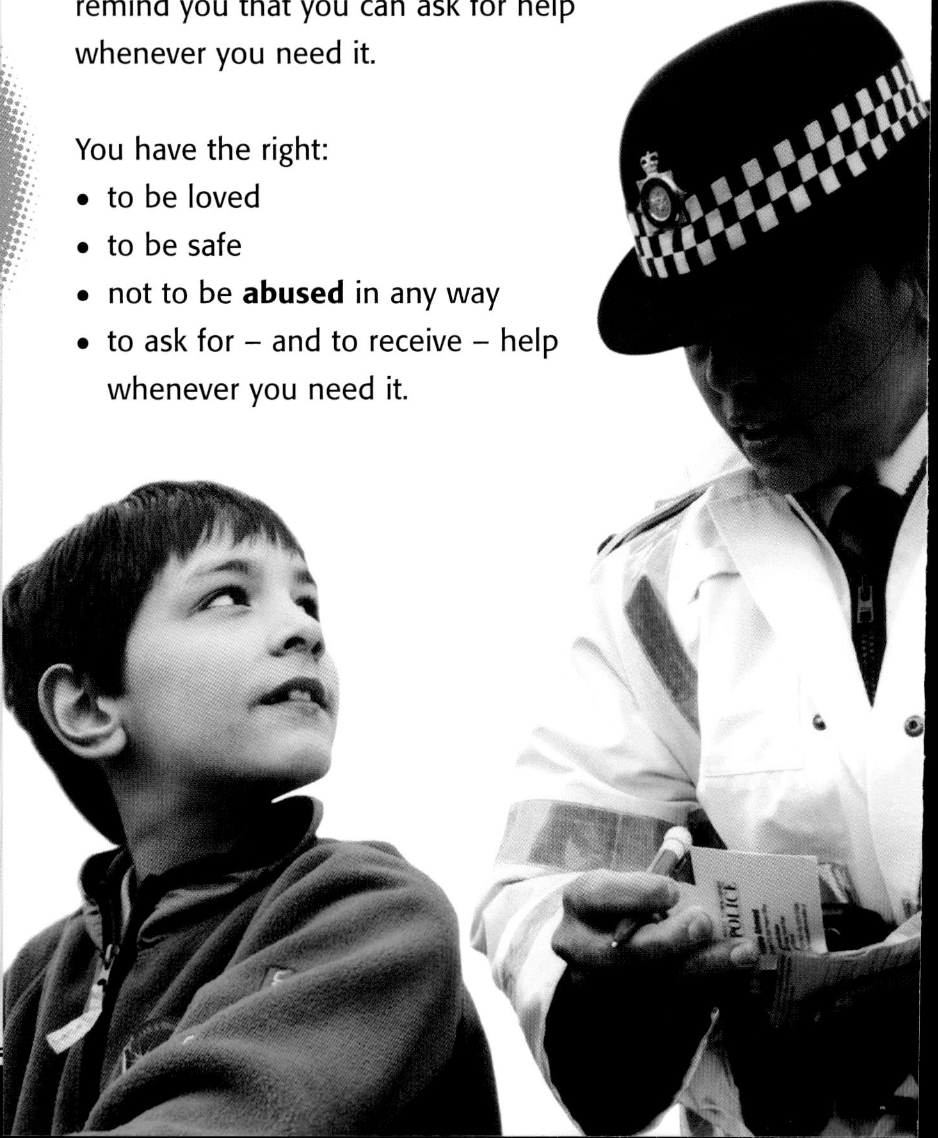

The police are there to help you in an emergency.

All children have the right to be treated well by others. With that comes the responsibility to treat others well, too.

Paying the price

We have seen that there are always **consequences** for doing wrong things at school and at home. People who break the law also get into trouble – with the police.

All kinds of violence are against the law, including **physical violence** and **domestic violence**. People who are violent may have to pay a **fine**, do unpaid work in the community or go to prison.

Lin's Story

Lin was in a gang who were always getting into trouble. Last year, she got caught by the police and had to do 100 hours of community work.

'Being punished made me grow up a bit. I could see that I was wrong. We used to assault and rob people. I just wanted to get easy money. Now I can see that I was really scaring and hurting people. If I could, I'd say sorry to them for punching them and kicking them.'

THINK IT THROUGH

Do children need special protection from violence by the law?

Yes. It is hard for children to look after themselves, so they do need special protection from the law.

No. Everyone has the same right to be safe from violence. The law should protect adults as much as children.

What do YOU think?

TOP TIPS

If you ever feel frightened that someone is about to hurt you or somebody else, you can phone the police for urgent help. See page 31 for how to do this.

Violence? No way!

What can you do to make the world a more peaceful place?

The world may have some violent people in it. However, most people would not wish to hurt anybody, and just want peace in the world. Many **organizations** around the world are working to bring violence to an end.

🔊 Staying close to your friends is a good way to keep safe when you are out.

Little and large

Some people have set up youth clubs in dangerous areas, so that young people can have fun and stay out of trouble. Many schools are finding ways to tackle **bullying**. There are also organizations to help children and adults who have been hurt by violence (see page 31).

Talk time

What would you do if someone threatened you?

Tanvi: I'd walk away as quickly as I could.

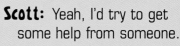

Scott: Yeah, I'd try to get some help from someone.

Lei-Lei: You need to stay really calm.

Rick: That's right. And maybe just say that you don't want any trouble.

Be safe, stay safe

There is a lot you can do to stay safe and to help to make the world a more peaceful place. Think about these ideas:

- Stay out of danger! Avoid walking in dark, lonely places – and always tell a trusted person where you are and who you are with.
- Be informed! Find out about who you can talk to and where you can get help if you need it (reading this book is a great start!).
- Talk, talk, talk! Tell someone you trust if you – or anyone you know – has been hurt or might be hurt. Try to talk to people about problems before they get too big.
- Protect yourself! If you can, take self-defence lessons. Or stay fit through sport and active games.
- Say 'No' to bullying! Treat other people kindly and fairly, and help them whenever you can.
- Do what you can to support organizations that are working to bring peace to the world.

Newsflash

Luisa decided she wanted to know how to defend herself if she was attacked:

'We've just been learning self defence at school. It's really interesting – and cool! We learned all the basic punches, kicks and blocks, and we've also been taught how to free your arm and neck if someone grabs you. If someone attacks you, you should shout 'Fire!', because then more people will come outside.'

Your family can help you to work out ways to stay out of danger.

THINK IT THROUGH

Can children really make a difference to violence in the world?

Yes. You can't do everything, but you can do little things – and every little helps.

No. Only adults can make a difference, because they are the ones who have the power.

What do YOU think?

Glossary

abuse when someone hurts or injures someone with physical or emotional violence

alcohol type of drink, such as beer or vodka, that can make people drunk because it contains a drug called ethanol

banned to make a rule or law to stop something happening

bully to pick on someone and treat them cruelly and unfairly

carer someone who looks after children but is not their parent

consequences results of a person's actions

domestic violence when one adult in a family uses violence against another adult in the home

drug any kind of chemical that has an effect on your body – changing the way you feel, think or act

emotional violence when nasty words and cruel behaviour are used to hurt someone

fine money someone has to pay as a punishment when they have broken a rule or law

government group of people who run a country

illegal against the law

law rules made by the government of a country, that must be obeyed

MP Member of Parliament; person who helps to run the country

media the places we find out information, such as newspapers, magazines, radio, TV and the Internet

organization large group of people all working together to achieve the same aims

peer pressure when friends try to get you to do something you would not normally do

physical violence when physical force, such as hitting or kicking, is used to hurt someone

professional when someone does something for their work

racism treating someone badly because of their race or religion

right something that is fair and that you can expect

threaten when someone scares someone else by saying that they will do something nasty to them in the future

victim someone who suffers because of the actions of somebody else

Check it out

Check out these books and websites to find out more about the issues raised in this book — and to get help and advice.

Books

Racism and Prejudice — Why Is It Wrong?
  Jane Bingham (Heinemann Library, 2005)

Bullies, Bigmouths & So-Called Friends,
  Jenny Alexander (Hodder, 2004)

Bullying — Why Does It Happen?,
  Sarah Medina (Heinemann, 2004)

Websites

ChildLine (UK): www.childline.org.uk

Kidscape (UK): www.kidscape.org.uk

Kids Help Line (Australia): www.kidshelp.com.au

How to phone the police

Remember — the police are there to help you. In an emergency, you should:

- Dial 999 from the UK. (Dial 000 from Australia.)
- Ask for the police.
- Tell the police:
  - where you are
  - why you need them
  - your name
  - the number of the phone you are calling from.

Help for adults

If there is domestic violence in your home, you may wish to tell the adults in your family that they can get help, too. Here are some places that adults can turn to:

Parentline Plus (UK): www.parentlineplus.org.uk; tel. 0808 800 2222

Citizens Advice Bureau (UK): www.citizensadvice.org.uk

Women's Aid (UK): www.womensaid.org.uk

Refuge (UK — for women and children): www.refuge.org.uk; tel. 0808 2000 247

For a list of helplines and organizations in Australia working against domestic violence, adults can contact:

www.padc.dpmc.gov.au

www.facs.gov.au

Getting help

If you feel very worried or upset about violence, you may need to talk to someone urgently. You can speak to an adult you trust, or you can phone a helpline for support.

- In the UK, you can phone ChildLine free on 0800 1111 (open 24 hours a day). Please remember that calls to 0800 numbers do not show up on phone bills. You can also write to them at ChildLine, Freepost NATN1111, London E1 6BR
- In Australia, you can phone Kids Help Line on 1800 55 1800 (open 24 hours a day).

Index

Titles in the *Get Wise* series include:

Hardback   0 431 21032 2

Hardback   0 431 21003 9

Hardback   0 431 21004 7

Hardback   0 431 21002 0

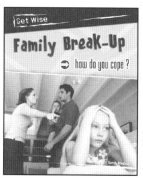

Hardback   0 431 21035 7

Hardback   0 431 21033 0

Hardback   0 431 21036 5

Hardback   0 431 21000 4

Hardback   0 431 21001 2

Hardback   0 431 21034 9

Find out about other titles from Heinemann Library on our website
www.heinemann.co.uk/library